The Bristol Year

Ancient and Modern City Traditions

by Maurice Fells

Illustrations by Nicki Bower

If readers would like to inform us of any other customs that they may know of, please contact Broadcast Books on:
0117 9238891

email to: Catherine@broadcastbooks.co.uk

Published by
Broadcast Books
c/o Clifton Bookshop,
84 Whiteladies Road
Bristol BS8 2QP
tel: 0117 9238891
email: catherine@broadcastbooks.co.uk
www.broadcastbooks.co.uk

Cover illustration: Nicki Bowers

Design: Sally Mundy
www.angelswing.co.uk

Printed in the UK by Cromwell Press, Trowbridge, Wilts.

Contents

Acknowledgments

As a Bristolian and journalist I wanted to share my love of the city and its heritage of traditions, in what is, I think, the first ever collection of information on the subject. Although this book does not set out to be the definitive guide to the city's tremendous wealth of customs, it celebrates the most famous of them as well as the new traditions taking shape all the time because of Bristol's exciting ethnic diversity. I hope that not only visitors but also established Bristolians will all find something unexpected and of interest in these pages.

This book could not have been written without the help of many people. However, special thanks must go to Alan Canterbury, Virger to the Lord Mayor of Bristol, who was extremely helpful in sharing with me his knowledge not only of the Lord Mayor's Chapel but also of civic affairs. The Reverend Des Tucker, a member of the Honorary Clergy team at St. Stephen's Church, City, (the 'city' distinguishes it from two other churches with the same name in the suburbs of Southmead and Soundwell) is not only a fount of information on Bristol's religious history but also of the city generally. Steven Ryan, Boardmaster of Queen Elizabeth's Hospital, was generous with his time and shared with me his passion for the school and its history.

Richard Harris and Andrew Gregg, both former Presidents of Bristol Law Society, were equally helpful in guiding me through the Society's fascinating and long history. Members of the staff at Bristol Central Library and Bristol Records Office were most patient in dealing with my numerous enquiries.

A special debt of gratitude is due to Janet Pritchard, a very good friend whose unfailing enthusiasm and suggestions greatly encouraged me in writing this book. Finally, very many thanks to Veronica Smith and Grace Cooper for invaluable additional checking and research.

Detail from a stained glass window
in the Lord Mayor's Chapel

Introduction

Few towns outside London have such a wealth of historic customs as Bristol. Perhaps this rich seam of its heritage should not be surprising as until the early 19th century it was the second city in the country after London, and many of its civic customs and ceremonies still closely follow those of the capital.

However, it is not only local authority events that provide a feast of colour and ceremony throughout the year. Many centuries-old traditions peculiar to schools, churches, professional bodies and charitable institutions in Bristol are still faithfully observed, enriching the city's calendar immeasurably.

Bristol was the first borough in the country that was granted county status by a Royal Charter of Edward III in 1373. The new county separated Bristol from Gloucestershire to the north and Somerset to the south. The King also gave Bristol the privilege of appointing a Sheriff, and the Mayor was given the right to have a sword carried in front of him at all civic occasions. Hence, the creation of the office of City Swordbearer, which still exists. This official is the only individual permitted to retain his headdress in the presence of royalty. His cap and sword symbolise inflexible justice, and the Mayor's right and readiness to defend the interests of the burgesses, or citizens, whenever necessary.

In 1542 Henry VIII created the Diocese of Bristol, making the county also a city. The lands and revenues of the Abbey of St. Augustine at College Green, which had been confiscated by Henry several years earlier during his Dissolution of the Monasteries, were now partially restored to endow the former Abbey's new status as the cathedral and bishopric of the city.

One of Bristol's most prestigious titles is that of "Freedom of the City". It dates back to Elizabethan times when the status of 'Freeman' was needed to be able to trade in the city or become a merchant. Citizens acquired this status by one of four different means, although it was also occasionally conferred as a gift. It was the automatic right of any  man who had served an apprenticeship and who had carried out business in the city for seven years, during which time he had to conduct himself soberly, could not frequent taverns or play dice. It could also be conferred if he were born in the city to a freeman; or if he married the daughter or widow of a freeman; or finally, if he paid a 'fine' to the city corporation. This amount varied between twelve to one hundred guineas, according to status and to the benefits that were likely to be derived. A byelaw of 1606 imposed a penalty of £100 on the Mayor and Chamberlain if they admitted anyone to the status of Freeman contrary to these conditions.

In 1835 the Municipal Corporation Act did away with the acquisition of the status of Freeman by paying 'fines'. 'Freedom of the City' is now a rare honour and today councillors put forward the names of those who have given "distinguished and eminent" service to the city for the title. The Freedom of Bristol has been granted to only 36 individuals since 1888.

Three new Freemen were admitted to the Roll of Honour early in 2003. They included the Rt. Reverend Barry Rogerson. He was Bishop of Bristol (the title is something of a misnomer for the diocese stretches from Avonmouth in the west to Swindon in the east) from 1985-2002. He ordained the first women priests into the Church of England at a special service in Bristol Cathedral in 1994.

The Labour Party veteran Tony Benn was recognised for his contribution to political life in Bristol during the 33 years he served the old Bristol South East constituency as its Member of Parliament. He was defeated in 1983 by the Conservative Party candidate after constituency boundary changes.

The third man to be honoured was Sir Jack Hayward, the former Midlands businessman now living in the Bahamas. In 1970 he rescued the rotting hulk of Isambard Brunel's ocean-going liner the *SS Great Britain* from Sparrow Cove in the Falkland Islands, where she had been beached for over a hundred years. Sir Jack financed the £150,000 project to float her on a special pontoon eight thousand miles back to the berth in Bristol docks, from where she had been launched in 1843. Since her return to the city Sir Jack has not only financed her restoration, but also contributed very substantially to the creation of Bristol's new Empire and Commonwealth Museum at Temple Meads.

Other Freemen of Bristol include the late Sir Winston Churchill. The former Prime Minister was granted the honour in 1943 when he was Chancellor of Bristol University. Five members of the Wills tobacco family were also given the title. They came from one of the city's wealthiest families and were involved in so many parts of its life. Amongst many other philan-thropic gifts the Wills family endowed the University of Bristol, the City Art Gallery and laid the foundation stones of thirty congregational churches.

The honour has also been conferred on the German city of Hanover, one of Bristol's 'twin'cities', on HMS Bristol, the guided missile warship, and on the Bristol District branch of the Merchant Navy Association. The Gloucestershire Regiment has been granted it twice, first in 1958 and again in 2002. By then the "Glorious Glosters", as they are nicknamed, had become part of the Royal Gloucestershire, Berkshire and Wiltshire Regiment following a round of military amalgamations announced by the

Ministry of Defence. On both occasions, the soldiers exercised their right to march through Bristol with bayonets fixed, drums beating and regimental flags flying.

New freemen sign the Roll of Honour at a meeting of the City Council which is open to the public and are presented with a citation by the Lord Mayor. Details of the ceremonies are publicised in the local papers.

Crowning the Queen of the Apples

The ancient custom of wassailing the apple trees to ensure a good crop the following autumn takes place on a Sunday towards the end of January in an orchard a few miles north of Bristol.

This ceremony was hosted by retired barrister Frank Buckley of Filton, who died in 2003. He first held it in 1953 in his orchard at Cribbs Causeway and ran it until 2002. Each year there were around 200 guests who attended by private invitation that Frank sent out with his Christmas card.

Wassailing is usually held at night but this event kicks-off at mid-day. Guests are welcomed with hot-punch and gingerbread around a blazing bonfire. An Apple Queen is chosen and crowned - her throne is usually a seat on a tractor.

The roots of the oldest apple tree are anointed with cider and the Apple Queen places a piece of toast in the branches for the wren and the robin. An old wassailing song is sung by Morris dancers and then shotguns are fired into the apple trees to drive away any pests and devils. Guests drink repeated toasts to Her Majesty the Queen, the Apple Queen and the trees.

The pagan festival of wassailing was one of the ancient rites inspired by early fertility gods. It was usually celebrated in apple growing regions - the West Country, Wales, Normandy and Brittany. Not only were apples grown in these areas but cider was the local drink rather than wine or beer. The word 'wassail' comes from two Anglo-Saxon ones meaning "good health". It is to be hoped that Frank Buckley's wassailing ceremony will continue in his memory.

 ## Past Traditions: Hospital Sunday

After the establishment of the National Health Service in 1948, the tradition of Hospital Sunday gradually petered out. But this vital tradition was certainly still in force during the early years of the 20th century. On the second Sunday on January, special sermons were read and collections made in the churches and chapels of the city, and the proceeds were donated to the Bristol General Hospital and Bristol Royal Infirmary.

The Bristol General Hospital is an impressive Italianate building near Bathhurst Basin. It was built in 1832 at a cost of £25,000 raised through public subscription, and re-built in 1858. The main benefactors were Joseph Easton and George Thomas.

The Bristol Royal Infirmary was one of the first public hospitals in England. It was opened in 1717 on a field known as Jobbin's Leaze, and attracted Royal Patronage in 1735. It was the first hospital outside London to support itself by voluntary contributions. One of its chief benefactors was John Elbridge, Deputy Comptroller of Customs, who bequeathed £5000 to its continued upkeep when he died in 1738. The building as it is seen today (once the 'cottage hospital') was begun in 1781, with various new additions swallowing up most of the houses and businesses in Marlborough Street and Upper Maudlin Street over the next two centuries. The "new" building on the other side of the road was opened by George V in 1912.

Late February

From Rags to Riches

Rag stands for "Raising and Giving" and over the years Bristol Rag Week has given many thousands of pounds to local charities. It is normally held in the last week of February.

Bristol University Students Rag Week is a time when almost anything can happen. This week-long extravaganza sees students taking part in a variety of madcap stunts ranging from attempting to drink pubs dry to racing in bath tubs full of baked beans. Undergraduates in fancy dress collect for Rag charities in the streets.

Crowds line the streets for the carnival-style procession on the final Saturday of Rag Week. Decorated float and foot parties representing the various university departments make up the parade,

probably the biggest fund-raiser of the week. It leaves The Downs at 2pm and crawls through the shopping streets of Clifton, into the city centre and Broadmead and back to the Students' Union headquarters in Queens Road, Clifton.

The Boys in Blue

The long bluecoats, yellow stockings and highly polished shoes worn by the boarders of Queen Elizabeth's Hospital have been a familiar part of the Bristol scene since the school was founded by John Carr in the 16th century.

Carr was the elder son of a Bristol alderman and merchant. He himself became a wealthy man making his living from manufacturing soap with factories in Bristol and Bow, London. Carr lived in what is now Baldwin Street, off the City Centre, and also owned five other properties, as well as inheriting several estates in North Somerset.

He died in 1586 aged 52 and left a substantial legacy to found Queen Elizabeth's Hospital as a school for orphans and poor boys of Bristol. Carr's instructions to his executors were that the school was to be modelled on Christ's Hospital, London, a school that had been set up for fatherless children and for those from poor homes.

17

On March 21 1590 Queen Elizabeth I granted Queen Elizabeth's Hospital (QEH) a charter confirming its title and rights. This document in Latin includes the school motto "Dum tempus habemus operemur bonum" - (Whilst we have time, let us do good). An illustration on the charter shows the Queen enthroned, delivering it to the Mayor and Aldermen of Bristol, who in their scarlet robes are kneeling before her. A number of boys in school dress are also pictured. The Charter concludes that "the hospital shall be everlasting and shall be named after her." This historic document is in safe keeping in the office of the school governors.

QEH opened in September 1590 with just twelve boys, after an existing building in Denmark Street near College Green was made suitable for its use. Much work was accomplished through the donations of several philanthropists, including the Mayor of Bristol, who gave £530. As the number of boys grew the school moved into a bigger building in Christmas Street. In 1847 the school moved to its present site high on the slopes of Brandon Hill, in a magnificent purpose-built mock-Tudor edifice. A dramatic flight of steps leads up from Jacobs Wells Road to the main entrance.

Boarders once wore large brass badges bearing the initials of various early benefactors - like JC - John Carr or MR - Lady Mary Ramsey. Lady Mary was the daughter of a Bristol merchant and widow of Sir Thomas Ramsey, once Lord Mayor of London. In 1601 she bequeathed the school £1,000. Both benefactors are remembered in the names of school houses.

The granting of the charter is remembered at a special service held on or near March 21 each year in Bristol Cathedral. Boarders wearing the school's traditional dress can be seen making their way down Park Street to the Cathedral for the Charter Day Service.

Queen Elizabeth's Hospital has close links with the Lord Mayor's Chapel. By tradition it provides the choir for Council Prayers when the Lord Mayor, Aldermen and Councillors attend a service before meetings of the council, and for the Mayor Making Service each May. Boarders regularly worship at the Chapel on Sundays and at special school services throughout the year.

April or Second Tuesday after Easter

The Tale of the Tuppeny Starvers

A mouth-watering tradition dating back more than 200 years takes place in Bristol on the second Tuesday after Easter. This is when pupils at St. Michael's School, Kingsdown, look forward to a break from lessons to be given big spicy buns, nine inches in diameter.

The distribution of these buns has its roots in a Feast for the Poor which the Churchwardens of St. Michael the Archangel on the Mount Without provided each year after they were elected. How the feast started is lost in the mists of time, but it must have been a costly burden on the wardens for it was open to all the poor in St. Michael's Parish.

Some relief came to the wardens through the good offices of Peter Davies and his wife Mary, who settled in the parish in the 18th century after arriving from Cardiganshire, Wales. They left money in their will to pay for the feast.

The tradition of the feast ended with the introduction of the Poor Laws in 1834 which were to help the needy with food and accommodation. Instead, the legacy of Peter Davies was diverted to pay for buns known as "Tuppeny Starvers", named after the cost of making them and their size, which was intended to banish starvation for a while! The buns were then distributed to local children.

Until St. Michael's Church closed in 1999, the buns were distributed by the Vicar, but this pleasant duty now falls upon the headteacher at St. Michael's school. The children troop into the parish hall on the second Tuesday after Easter to collect their confection.

Former Traditions: St. David's Day at St. Michael's Church

Although Peter Davies, a wealthy Bristol businessman, lived in Kingsdown for forty years in the early part of the eighteenth century, his passion for Wales never diminished. On his death he made a bequest for a candlelight service to be held in St. Michael's Church on the Sunday nearest to St. David's Day - March 1. He provided thirty shillings (£1.50) to pay for the preacher, and twelve shillings and threepence (61 pence) for the candles. The service included hymns written by Welshmen, with the lesson read in Welsh, and the Lord's Prayer also said in Welsh. This service started during the 1750s and was held each year until the church closed.

St. Michael's Church now stands neglected in an unkempt churchyard, with its windows partly covered by board or obscured by rampant ivy. Unfortunately, it has become a target for vandals. The church is one of the oldest in the city. The original date is pre-1148 and the 'Without' in its title indicates it was originally outside the Bristol city wall. It was rebuilt in the 15th century and once more around 1775, but the 15th century tower remained. The church stands on St. Michael's Hill, a highway itself steeped in history. It was up this hill, one of the ancient roads leading out of Bristol to the River Severn, that Protestant Marian Martyrs climbed to be burned at the stake at the very top, where now Cotham Church stands.

 ## Bristol International Animation Festival

With the phenomenal success of Nick Parks' animated creations, best known through the Wallace and Gromit films of Aardman productions, Bristol has rapidly become a national and international focus for animation. Since 1999 the city has hosted an International Animation Festival, described as "the Cannes of the Animated World" each April. It is based at the Watershed Cinema and arts complex, Cannon's Marsh. Apart from screenings of the latest creations from the world of animated film, which culminate in a party and the awarding of the Cartoon d'Or, Europe's major animation prize, visitors can also take part in a wide variety of activities, celebrations, lectures and masterclasses.

Details from: info@animatedencounters.org.uk, tel: 0117 9275102

May Day

May Day has long been an occasion for much merry-making. The best known of the celebrations is probably that of dancing around the maypole. This may no longer be happening on every village green but a sturdy pair of legs - and a head for heights - is still needed if you wish to join the choristers of St. Stephen's Church in St. Stephens St, just off Corn St, who greet the first day of May in grand style.

This ancient church was once a tiny chapel, of which now only one tomb and a small piece of sunken floor remains. It was an outpost of the Benedictine monastery at Glastonbury, twenty miles away to the south east of the city. Even today the parish boundaries are unusual because they stretch out to the Severn Estuary to take in the islands of Steep Holm and Flat Holm.

When the river Frome was diverted in the 13th century, creating the harbour, the city of Bristol began to increase its trading wealth dramatically. St. Stephen's stood on the quayside of the harbour, and old paintings show the ships moored so close to the church as to be almost touching its walls. Now that the old harbour has been filled in, St. Stephen's Church ministers to the busy workers and shoppers of the commercial heart of the city, but its lovely façade and peaceful churchyard are almost hidden behind the offices of Corn St. The interior is airy, bright and graceful, with noteworthy tombs and other points of architectural interest, including an embossed, gilded ceiling and stained glass windows.

The glory of St. Stephen's is its 15th century tower, which rises 133 feet without the pinnacles above the busy heart of the city. It was paid for by the wealthy merchant John Shyppard in 1470, and built by the master mason Benet Crosse. On at 7am on May Day morning the Rector of Bristol and members of the *Antient (sic) Society of St. Stephen's Ringers* climb the tower. (Also see November). After singing hymns and madrigals at the top of the tower, and occasionally ringing out the twelve bells, the assembled gathering negotiates its way back down the spiral stone staircase of the perpendicular tower for a hearty breakfast in the church's Common Room. The tradition is thought to follow that of the choir at Magdalen College, Oxford, which welcomes the month of May from the college's Great Tower.

Apart from the *Antient Society of Ringers of St. Stephens*, which is in reality a philanthropic society of local businessmen dedicated to the maintenance and enhancement of the church, St. Stephen's also has a nationally famous society of handbell ringers, ringing twelve bells, the St. Stephen's Ringers. They practice every Monday evening and can be heard before the service each Sunday. They also ring at Christchurch at the top of Corn Street.

The May Day Service normally starts at 7.00 am. Members of the public are welcome to join the congregation.

 ## The Ringer's Café

Donations from members of the Antient Society enabled the Church Common Room to be refurbished and re-opened as The *Ringer's Café* in 2000. It is open to the public for home-made breakfasts, soups, cakes and snacks from 10am - 2pm.

Details of the service, and other ceremonial services throughout the year, from St. Stephen's Church parish office, tel: 0117 9277977 or email: enquiries@ststephensbristol.co.uk

Jack-in-the-Green

Bristol's herald of summer is a lively and colourful character known as Jack-in-the-Green. He stands nine feet tall and is covered in greenery and flowers and leads a lively procession through the streets of the city. This symbol of fertility is accompanied by about two dozen attendants, also completely clothed in green rags and vegetation.

Jack only appears once a year, on the first Saturday in May. He sets off from Narrow Quay in the City Docks (from outside the Arnolfini arts centre). He and his followers play various musical instruments, and sing and dance. The revellers head for Broadmead, weaving around the shoppers, and then climb up St. Michael's Hill and into the suburbs of Kingsdown, Redland and Horfield.

More than five hours after leaving the City Docks, and partaking of suitable refreshments at hostelries en route, Jack and his followers eventually arrive at Horfield Common. Here Jack is stripped of his foliage to release the spirit of summer.

No one knows for sure how this curious ritual started although Jack in the Green processions were commonplace across England about two hundred years ago. Bristol is now one of the few cities which still carries on with the tradition.

Brushing up on Art

The Bristol Savages is a society founded in 1904 so that artists and like-minded people might "meet, sketch and converse together in a convivial atmosphere". They first met in private studios but in 1919 bought the Red Lodge, a large Elizabethan House on Park Row, as their headquarters. A lease was drawn up after which the Savages formally handed over the building to the City of Bristol. Since then the artists have met here weekly during seven months of the year.

The Savages respect the diversity of cultures from all over the world and those of the Native American tribes play a large part in their traditions. Their studio, in an annexe built in the garden of the Red Lodge, is known as the "Wigwam" and is designed on the lines of an old tithe barn.

Each "brother" Savage wears a lapel badge, and either a red, blue or green feather. The colours distinguish between artists, entertaining members which include singers and raconteurs, and lay members. The feathers are held in a pin badge made from an American five-cent coin. To this day guests are formally welcomed with a toast and a traditional Sioux greeting.

Before the evening's entertainment, which is provided by members, the artists enjoy a sketching session on a subject chosen by the chairman of the session. The drawings are later exhibited in the Wigwam for inspection and informal discussion.

In the first two weeks of May the Savages stage their annual exhibition. The works on show are not the two-hour sketches made at the weekly meetings but the result of many hours of painstaking work. The exhibition is open to the public and admission is free.

Further details from the Red Lodge, tel: 0117 9211360.

Mayor Making

Long before Bristol became a county in the fourteenth century it had appointed its own Mayor, a title deriving from the Latin "civis major", meaning Chief Citizen. The first person to hold the post of Mayor was Roger Cordewaner in 1216, and the last was Herbert Ashman in 1898. A year later after granting the city the right to have a Lord Mayor, as opposed to a mere Mayor, the eighty year old Queen Victoria visited Bristol and knighted Herbert Ashman on the steps of the old Council House in Corn Street. He then became the first Lord Mayor a year later. The title of Lord Mayor is the gift of the monarch, and only two dozen cities in the United Kingdom have it.

The Mayor of Bristol has the right to take his seat on the bench of any law court in the land. When John Noble was Mayor of Bristol in 1762 he decided to claim this right on a visit to London, and took his seat in the Court of Admiralty. The Judge was taken aback and was about to have him ejected until he was informed that Noble was privileged by charter to exercise this right. His Lordship graciously offered Noble a seat beside him, whereupon Noble rose, bowed and announced that having asserted his right he would at once withdraw - which must have irritated everyone all the more.

"Lord Mayor's Day" is normally the third Tuesday in May, with the Mayor-making ceremony in the Council Chamber of the

Council house on College Green. The new incumbent, who usually holds office for one year, must be a councillor, and is elected by his or her colleagues at their annual meeting. The name of each Mayor and Lord Mayor since 1216 is engraved on a wall in the Conference Room of the Council House.

Before the meeting, councillors wearing their scarlet robes process from the Council House to St. Mark's Chapel across Park St., for a service. This beautiful small church, sandwiched between the shops of Park St. is better known as the Lord Mayor's Chapel. It is the only place of worship in the country owned and maintained by a local authority.

The Chapel was founded in 1230 as a hospital tending the sick, feeding the poor and providing schooling. After the Dissolution the Corporation bought it for £1,000. Between 1687 and 1722 exiled French Huguenots living in Bristol prayed here, but since then it has been the official church for the Mayor and councillors.

Prior to the early 18th century the Mayor and his councillors had attended Bristol Cathedral, but had a falling out with the clergy there. This came about because the civic dignitaries were in the habit of leaving services before the hour-long sermon was preached, and in doing so not only snubbed the preacher but also caused a commotion.

The Lord Mayor's official regalia dates from medieval times and comprises a scarlet robe edged in fur, a feathered tricorn hat, gauntlets and gold chain of office, which alone weighs nearly three pounds. Scarlet is a royal colour and was worn way back in 1415 to denote authority from the king. On occasions the Lord Mayor is expected to wear velvets and a dress sword, the correct outfit three centuries ago for men of distinction appearing at Court.

Bristol's Lord Mayor is one of only five in England and Wales who can be addressed as "The Right Honourable", and Bristol is

Detail from a window in the
Lord Mayor's Chapel

the only city outside London that has a State Coach for its leading citizen. An official residence - the Mansion House on The Promenade, Clifton - is also provided. This imposing home with 22 rooms was built in 1874 by Alderman Thomas Proctor for his own use, but seven years later he gave it to the city. Everyone from The Queen to showbusiness personalities have been entertained here while on official visits to the city.

The role of Lord Mayor is now very much a ceremonial one, with its holder attending about one thousand events each year ranging from church fetes to conferences and from prize-giving ceremonies to Christmas carol services.

Access details: Members of the public can sit in the public gallery for the Mayor Making ceremony. Space is limited so it is best to contact the council's Press Office beforehand on 0117 9222650.

 Former Traditions: The Lord Mayor's Tram

A custom which ended just before the Second World War was The Lord Mayor's Tram. This was a vehicle beautifully decorated with strings of coloured lights. It would drive slowly around the city streets to raise money for gifts of food and presents for the poor children of Bristol.

The Rush Sunday Service

There's a chance to re-live the splendour of medieval costumes and ceremony when a centuries-old tradition is kept alive each Whit Sunday amid the glorious architecture of St. Mary Redcliffe, which Queen Elizabeth I is reputed to have declared as "the fairest, goodliest and most famous parish church in England". It may be more than 500 years old but the Rush Sunday service is still the most spectacular event in the Bristol calendar. The service takes its name from the rushes, freshly picked from the Somerset Levels, which are strewn across the floor, in keeping with ancient custom.

The first Rush Sunday service was instigated in 1494 by William Spenser, a Mayor of Bristol. In an attempt, perhaps, to get his councillors to church more often to pray for his soul, Spencer made provision in his will for "three priests sufficiently instructed in sacred divinity to preach the word of God" on the Monday, Tuesday and Wednesday after the Feast of Pentecost. They were to be paid 6s 8d each. The Mayor was also to be given 3s 4d each day to entertain the preacher to dinner. Remarkably, down the centuries the format of the service has changed little, apart from cutting the three sermons to just one on Pentecost, also known as WhitSunday, which happened at the time of the Reformation.

To mark the beginning of the Rush Sunday service today, the Lord Mayor, Lady Mayoress and City Swordbearer wearing his Cap of Maintenance (a furry

Cossack-style piece of headgear dating back to Elizabethan days) arrive from the Mansion House in an open horse-drawn carriage. They are accompanied by a mounted police escort.

The Lord Mayor enters the church through its Great West door to a fanfare sounded by liveried City Trumpeters, whose role dates back to the 17th century. Aldermen and City Councillors make a splash of colour in their scarlet robes as they follow the Lord Mayor, preceded by police constables with their silver maces glinting in the springtime sunshine. Her Majesty's Coroner for Avon and the High Sheriff follow in outfits that could have been borrowed from a Gilbert and Sullivan opera, and the procession then makes its stately way down the nave of the church.

Churchwardens and members of St. Mary Redcliffe Vestry are in Morning Dress, and the stewards who usher the congregation to their seats all sport red buttonhole carnations. A nosegay - or posy - of flowers is placed in each pew in front of the civic dignitaries. They take the posies with them after the service, following a medieval tradition when such posies were carried to ward off the evil smells of the streets.

The sermon is always preached by the Vicar of St. Mary Redcliffe. In 2003 the Reverend Tony Whatmough delivered his eleventh Rush Sunday Sermon. He is paid the princely sum of £1.89.by Bristol City Council. The money originally came from rental income on property that Spencer owned, but no records can be found to explain why and when the charge devolved on the council. The preacher is still entertained to lunch at the Mansion House after the service.

Tickets for the service can be obtained from St. Mary Redcliffe Parish office, tel: 0117 9291487

Remembering the Merchant Prince

William Canynges the Younger, a 15th century merchant who did so much to beautify the architectural gem of St. Mary Redcliffe Church, is specially remembered each July. This is when members of the Canynges Society hold their annual meeting, followed by a special service in the church.

Canynges (1402-1474) was a shipbuilder by trade who built up a business empire that made him not only Bristol's biggest employer, with eight hundred men on the payroll, but also the wealthiest merchant in town. This merchant prince lived in Redcliffe Street and poured much of his wealth into restoring Redcliffe Church, after the destruction of the spire in 1446. Canynges is said to have added the magnificent clerestory or upper-storey windows. Shortly after his wife died he gave up all his worldly possessions and trained for Holy Orders. He was ordained as a priest in 1468, at the age of 66. The Canynges Society, or Friends of St. Mary Redcliffe, was formed in 1848 in order to raise funds for the restoration of the church. Over the years it has made many substantial contributions to the restoration and maintenance of the church, ranging from repairs to the spire to providing individual lights on the choirstalls.

Around the time of the annual meeting the president, who holds office for a year, launches a fund-raising appeal amongst members. Many of them attend the Society's annual service when the sermon is delivered by a guest preacher. It is normally held early on the evening of the first Wednesday in July, although on several recent occasions it has taken place on a Sunday. Details from St. Mary Redcliffe Parish Office tel: 0117 9291487

The annual St. Paul's Carnival is Britain's biggest street carnival outside of Notting Hill, London, and is the climax of a festival week of cultural and sporting events.

The first carnival in 1967 was something of a modest affair, and began as a celebration of black and Irish culture in St. Pauls. Over the next three decades its flavour became more pronouncedly Caribbean, while involving all local schools and community groups in the area. Children from a dozen primary schools are attired in fantastically inventive and colourful self-made costumes, and dance in formation behind a series of floats playing live music, including drummers and Caribbean steel bands.

The carnival procession sets off from Portland Square in the early afternoon and slowly snakes its way along a circular route around City Road. After the parade the carnival moves to the main stage in the centre of St. Pauls', where prizes for best costumes and dancing are awarded. There are activities for children, music, craft and food stalls selling delicious barbequed

jerk chicken and goat, among other delicacies. Music plays out at every street corner. The party continues into the early hours, but the best family fun is recommended during the afternoon. The annual carnival today attracts around 20,000 visitors from around Britain as well as Bristol.

Details can be obtained from the carnival office, tel: 0117 9444176.

Degrees of Success

Standing sentinel-like at the top of Park Street and looking down over the centre of the city is the majestic tower of Bristol University. This 215 foot high tower dominates the main university building and houses Bristol's largest bell - Great George, weighing ten tons - which strikes the hour and tolls the death of monarchs and chancellors of the university.

The tower, the official name of which is the Wills Memorial Building, owes its origins to the generosity of Henry Overton Wills, who had given £100,000 towards endowing the university.

University College, Bristol, was founded in 1876 as a result of the genrosity of Henry Overton Wills, a Bristol entrepreneur whose fortune had been made in tobacco. He gave £100,000 in his will towards the endowment of a University for Bristol and the West of England. Henry became the University's first Chancellor. The Bristol Medical School which had been established forty-three years earlier eventually became part of it. In 1909 the college combined with the Merchant Venturers Technical College to

33

become the University of Bristol, and that year was granted a Royal Charter by King Edward VII. University College was the first higher education institution in England to admit women on an equal basis to men.

Several years later Henry's sons, George and Henry Herbert, further endowed the University for a new building to be built as a memorial to their father: the Wills Memorial Building and Tower, for which no expense was to be spared.

The Wills tower was designed in the Gothic style by the University's architect, Sir George Oatley, a Bristolian. It was opened in 1925 by King George V and Queen Mary. It is through the base of the tower that thousands of students pass each July to enter the Great Hall for a ceremony that formally marks the end of their university careers, as they receive their degrees.

All graduands of Bristol University must wear the regulation gown and hood relating to the degree which is to be conferred on them. Eleven different degree congregations are held in the second week of July. It is a time when the University of Bristol also awards honorary degrees to people of local, national and international distinction. However, the degree ceremonies are primarily occasions for students and their families who can be seen afterwards posing for photographs outside the Wills Memorial Building.

Music Fit for a Mayor

Two teenagers are chosen each summer to keep alive a musical tradition dating back to the 16th century. The Lord Mayor bestows upon each youngster the title of "City Wait" - a one year term of office during which the holder can be called upon to play at civic functions. In medieval times the City Wait was a minstrel who provided entertainment on civic occasions. The position died out during the 19th century but was revived in 1988 by the Guild of Guardians, a group of businessmen formed to support the office of the Lord Mayor.

Besides the historic title the Waits, chosen from schools in the city, are also given a financial award to help them pursue their music studies.

Showcase for Talent

Ashton Court Mansion and its glorious acres of woodland and meadows where deer herds roam, is situated just outside the city boundary, across the Clifton Suspension Bridge. It had been in the ownership of the wealthy Smyth family of landowners for 400 years, but to meet death duties when the last Smyth died in 1946 the estate was compulsorily purchased by the Bristol City Council. Although parts of the land were soon shorn off to accommodate the University of the West of England College of Art (Bower Ashton) and Ashton Park Comprehensive School, 840 acres remained to become what is perhaps the city's most beautiful and enjoyable asset. In 1959 the Council also acquired the dilapidated mansion, which had been long since stripped of its treasures, panelling and even roof leading. Since it came under council ownership it has been extensively renovated and is now a popular venue for conferences, weddings and banquets.

The estate is now the setting for numerous open-air events including the internationally famous Balloon Festival (see under August), and the two-day Orange Ashton Court Festival each July. This showcases a wealth of talent from local bands to nationally acclaimed musicians, playing on two main stages and in several marquees. There are also marquees devoted to film, theatre, dance and poetry.

The entertainment that is on offer is so diverse that the festival attracts 150,000 people - everyone from students to families. Over the weekend some 150 different acts will be appearing. Children are not forgotten either with the provision of a fairground, and there are well over 100 stalls selling everything from food to handmade crafts.

The Ashton Court Festival began after a handful of local music fans had been to the Windsor Free Festival, and thought Bristol should host something similar. They were given permission by the City Council and the first event was staged in 1974. The organisers relied on financial support from local shops and firms until Orange became the main sponsor in 2002.

The Festival Office (0117 9042275) will have details of concert times.

Harbour Festival makes a Splash

The well-known phrase "All Shipshape and Bristol Fashion" comes from the city's great maritime history, meaning everything was stowed and the ship ready to sail, and derives from Bristol's reputation for efficiency.

Bristol's docks and trade were the key to her fortunes since Roman times, when the Romans selected the city on the Avon with such easy land access to the rest of Britain as one of their most important military and commercial ports. Vestiges of their occupation can still be seen at Sea Mills, and in their defensive works on the heights of Clifton Down. Bristol ships and men were well represented at the siege of Calais in 1346, when 23 ships and 608 men were supplied to Edward III. After the Cabot voyages at the close of the late fifteenth century the city's trade in tobacco, silks, wine wood and - most notoriously - slaves, grew dynamically. However the gradual silting up of the Avon coupled with the ever-increasing size of trading vessels caused the city's docks to decline during the nineteenth century, with all activity re-routed at last to the docks at Portishead and Avonmouth. Since then the city centre docks were increasingly moribund and were closed completely to commercial shipping in the 1970s.

In the last three decades The Bristol Docks area has been revitalised as a leisure area for the citizens of Bristol, with many waterside bars and restaurants, a museum, two arts centres and cinemas. The graceful Pero's footbridge named after a slave brought to Bristol from the Caribbean in 1783, was opened to span the water in 1999.

The waterway itself has become the venue for the annual SWEB Bristol Harbour Festival, an extravagant celebration of the city's maritime heritage. The Lord Mayor takes to the water to officially open the festival by sailing in the Harbour Master's Launch from Cumberland Basin to St. Augustine's Reach. Hundreds of visiting sailing craft bedecked with brightly coloured flags moor in the City Docks for the next two days of water-based activities, attended by leading sportsmen and women several hundred thousand spectators.

Regular highlights include helicopter displays by the Royal Navy who demonstrate a winch rescue in the Floating Harbour. Raft and rowing races, sailing lessons for children, water canon displays and a tug-of-war involving naval cadets are also featured. Visiting ships include Royal Navy Vessels and historic sailing ships and schooners from Britain and Europe.

The harbour festival takes place on the first weekend in August. All the events are free. Details and times of specific events can be obtained from the events office, tel: 0117 9223719

The Sky's the Limit

In the warm, still evenings of summer it is now a familiar sight to see huge hot-air balloons floating high over the city skyline. Bristol has become world centre for this sport, and for the last twenty-five years it has hosted an annual international balloon

Fiesta every August. Don Cameron, Bristol owner of a small balloon manufacturing business, hatched the idea for such a festival in 1978 over a pint in a pub. He decided to create an event that would attract balloonists from all over the world. With organisational and financial help from the Bristol Junior Chamber, and sponsorship from local businesses, one weekend the following year a small gathering of balloonists met to celebrate what was to become Bristol's first balloon fiesta, when spectators watched the first mass ascent of 27 balloons mainly from the West Country, but also from Luxembourg, Ireland and West Germany.

From this small beginning the Fiesta has grown year after year. The Bristol International Balloon Fiesta is now in the top ten of public events in the United Kingdom and is featured on television programmes around the world, and Don Cameron's firm has now become the world's largest maker of hot-air balloons. It created a balloon in 2002 for the adventurer Steve Fossett, who became the first man to fly solo around the world.

These days around half a million people attend the four-day event held in the rolling parklands of the Ashton Court estate, just over the Clifton Suspension Bridge. They now watch nearly 150 balloons from dozens of countries lift off in the twice-daily mass ascents, weather permitting, to float gently away over the surrounding countryside at anything from 500 to 1,500 feet. The mass ascents normally take place between 6 and 7am and 6 and 7pm each day of the Fiesta. The remarkable balloon shapes include cans of beer, houses, a telephone, Rupert Bear and a giant fire extinguisher. Many balloons are now sponsored by businesses.

A major attraction now is the night-time balloon glow held on the Thursday before the Fiesta opens, when balloons are inflated and their burners lit in time to music. There is also a huge firework display. In the following days further entertainment is provided by funfairs, bands and shows. Admission is free. A few days before the fiesta half a dozen balloons, with the Lord Mayor in one of them, lift off from College Green for a breakfast time flight to publicise the event.

Further information from: www.bristolfiesta.co.uk or tel: 0117 9535884

Bristol International Kite Festival

Civilizations around the world have been flying kites for celebratory, pleasurable or military purposes for over 2500 years. Bristol's breezy open green spaces are ideal for this lovely sport, and the city has been hosting its international kite festival for the last seventeen years. The Festival takes place at the end of August at Ashton Court, and attracts over 70,000 visitors each year. It provides a great family day out as well as a showcase for some of the world's leading flyers, designers and kite makers from as far afield as Australia and New Zealand. The Festival has something to offer spectators and enthusiasts of all ages; from the brute power of man-lifting kite surf wings to the deft manoeuvring of delicate paper Indian fighters, and is a showcase for traditional and modern designs. Other attractions include flying animals and sea creatures, a Japanese fighting kite competition, kite making workshops for children, and a wind orchestra.

Details from the organisers, tel: 0117 9772002 Fax: 0117 9774255 info@abc-pr.co.uk www.kite-festival.org

September

Bristol in Full Bloom on the Downs

Another glorious green space that enhances the city is known as The Downs, often referred to today as Bristol's "green lung". They lie in the north-west of the city, at the top of Blackboy Hill, and comprise of four hundred acres of open and wooded country. Three hundred years ago this was a dangerous and desolate place, frequented by highwaymen, and the site of a gibbet where murderers were left twisting in the wind. One of the most notorious was Shenkin Protheroe, an ill-formed dwarf who lurked about ingratiating himself with kind-hearted passing travellers, who he would then attack and rob. On one occasion, his victim died as a result of the attack. Protheroe was caught and hung on the gibbet on the highest point of the Downs, in 1783, and is believed to haunt the spot ever after.

The Downs today have a much sunnier reputation and are a well-loved destination for walkers, lovers, sunbathers, kite flyers, footballers, cricketers and picnickers - although recently, to some annoyance, portable summer barbeques have been banned. Fairs and children's festivals are also occasionally permitted.

Until 1861 the land was in the ownership of the Society of Merchant Venturers and The Lords of the Manor of Henbury. However, the Society was anxious that the area should be made available for the pleasure and recreation of the public forever, and gave its share to the City Council. The Lords of the Manor of Henbury disposed of their share to the council for £15,000. The Downs Committee, made up of six members of the Society of Merchant Venturers and six city councillors, now look after the entire area.

At the end of August or beginning of September each year the Downs host The Bristol Flower Show. There are classes to cater for both professional and amateur gardeners, featuring garden tools, fruits, vegetables, sub-tropical and greenhouse plants and allotment produce. The show is regarded as one of the best in the West with entries in about 1,000 classes. Apart from the flowers and garden produce there are also country displays and local crafts stalls.

The first recorded flower show took place on July 2nd 1836 at "Mr Miller's" - presumably his house - "Durdham Down". During the following decades horticultural shows were held at the Clifton Zoo gardens, but they petered out due to lack of financial support in 1878. Another Flower Society had been formed in 1863, which put on a Spring and Winter Show, initially at the former Rifle Drill Hall which was next to the Museum and Art Gallery in Queen's Rd, but this was later transferred to the Victoria Rooms, presumably when the Hall was demolished to make way for the building of the University. The Winter Show in late autumn specialised in chrysanthemums and fruit, and the Spring show on flowers.

Open Doors Day

On Open Doors Day, every September, there's a chance to see inside some of Bristol's most fascinating and historically important buildings which are not normally open or fully accessible to the public. Bristol was one of the first cities in 1994 to stage this scheme that has now been adopted nationally. In its first year just twenty-eight buildings took part, now the number is more than double that.

Bank buildings with fine interiors, churches, offices in restored Georgian houses, caves and even a sewage treatment works all throw their doors open to an estimated 50,000 visitors each year. All the buildings are open from 10am until 4pm. One of the most popular attractions are the old mine workings at Redcliffe Caves, where long queues of visitors quickly form.

The day is organised by the Bristol Chamber of Commerce and Initiative, Bristol Architecture Centre and Bristol City Council. Details from the Bristol City Council website:

www.visitBristol.co.uk. To visit Redcliffe Caves, contact Alan Gray via www.bristoltours.com or e: toursandresearch@yahoo.com

Remembering Raja Rammohun Roy

A beautiful grade II listed funeral monument made of Bath stone in one of Bristol's cemeteries is an important place of pilgrimage for people from all over the world. This is the final resting place of Raja Rammohun Roy, regarded as the founder of modern India. Every autumn scores of visitors from the Indian sub-continent process to the shrine, completed in 1844 by William Princep, to pay homage to their great compatriot.

Raja Rammohun Roy was a Brahmin born in Bengal in 1772. He was a man of extraordinary gifts. He spoke many languages, including English, Persian, Hebrew, Greek and Latin, published newspapers and wrote many books on subjects ranging from grammar to geometry. But his great mission was to campaign for education for all and for other social reforms for his people, which he thought could flow from the establishment of a universal Indian religion. He championed women's rights and campaigned for the abolition of 'sati', by which Hindu widows throw themselves onto the funeral pyre of their husbands. In 1833 he visited Bristol, but after ten days in the city was taken ill with meningitis, and died. At first he was buried in the grounds of Beech House, Stapleton Grove, where he had been a guest. But ten years later a friend had him re-interred in Arnos Vale Cemetery, four years after it opened. Roy is also honoured by a statue, created by a leading Calcutta sculptor, which was unveiled outside the Central Library, College Green, in 1997.

Arnos Vale Cemetery is set on a hillside rising from the A4 Bristol to Bath Road at Brislington. It is a place of wild romantic greenery, and contains many other monuments of architectural merit. It is open every day, admission free. The pilgrimage takes place on September 27.

October

Legal Eagles on Parade

The start of the Michaelmas Law Term, or the new Legal Year is marked by the Legal Sunday Service at Bristol Cathedral. Judges from the High Court, Bristol Crown Court, barristers, solicitors all bewigged and wearing gowns in a colour appropriate to their professional status, along with High Sheriffs, Under Sheriffs, magistrates and court clerks, join the Lord Mayor for this annual service. It is normally held on the second Sunday in October. Shortly before the service starts at 11.15am, the legal luminaries can be seen processing from the Council House to the cathedral in all their finery.

45

The Lord Mayor is greeted by a trumpet fanfare when he reaches the Cathedral's North Door where the Dean of Bristol welcomes him. After the service, which ends with the National Anthem, the lawyers process back to the Council House for refreshment. It is fitting that the legal profession in Bristol is honoured with such pageantry, for the city is distinguished by having the oldest Law Society in the country. This was established in 1770 and is senior to the national Law Society by 55 years. The Bristol society's first meeting was held in the Bush Tavern, on the site of what is now the Lloyds TSB Bank in Corn Street. One of the early rules stipulated that meetings should start at "seven o'clock in the evening and continue until half an hour after ten, when the Tavern Bill should be called for and discharged."

The organisation was unique in Bristol at the time as it was the only society of professional men gathered mainly for professional business. The oldest surviving legal practice in England, Latchams, Montague, Niblett, opened its doors for business in 1710 in Stokes Croft. It has now moved offices and is merged with another firm. They are now Gregg, Latcham, Quinn.

Details of the service from the Bristol Cathedral office, tel: 0117 9264879

Church with the Nelson Touch

Lord Nelson's victory in the Battle of Trafalgar, 1805, may be the stuff of childhood history but it's not a date found in many diaries. However, this national hero who first went to sea at the age of 12, and lost his right eye and right arm in the French revolutionary wars, is not forgotten at St. Stephen's, City, a church with long maritime links. After the historic battle when Nelson won his victory against the French and Spanish fleets at Trafalgar, the church received a legacy to pay for a sermon to be

preached each year to mark the occasion. The Trafalgar Day Service has been held uninterruptedly since 1806, and takes place at 11am on the Sunday nearest Trafalgar Day - October 21. Members of various maritime organisations including the Royal Naval Reserve and Royal Marine Reserve take part in this service.

Details of the service from St. Stephen's Church parish office, tel: 0117 9277977 or email: enquiries@ststephensbristol.co.uk

November

All Saints Day

November is a particularly busy month for traditions. On All Saints Day - November 1 - a Christian festival in honour of all the saints, the Lord Mayor, former Lord Mayors, Honorary Aldermen and councillors attend a Communion Service at the Lord Mayor's Chapel. Although records indicate they have been doing this since at least the 1720's no one knows why the tradition started. Afterwards those present adjourn to the Mansion House for breakfast, the cost of which is borne by an anonymous benefactor.

Ringing the Changes

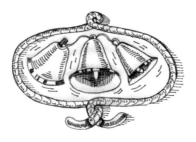

When Queen Elizabeth I visited Bristol on one of her royal progresses around her realm, the bells of St. Stephen's Church pealed out to greet her from their beautiful, soaring tower, which had been completed in 1470, around two hundred years before. (See May Day). She was so impressed by the sound that she promised the bell ringers a royal warrant. The warrant never quite materialised, but over the following centuries the church's bell ringers, known as the *Antient Society of Ringers of St. Stephen's*, developed an increasing sense of their special status. Unlike the presumably more soberly behaved ringers from other churches in the city, the St. Stephen's Ringers became a sort of neo hell-fire group, a magnet for well-to-do rakes and young bloods, who combined ringing and general carousing in a way that the old Queen may not have quite intended.

By the eighteenth century *The Antient Society of Ringers* and the faithful actual ringers of St. Stephen's bells had diverged into completely different groups, but it was not until the 1890s that the *Antient Society* was finally brought into line by the Rector of St. Stephen's. He refused to allow the name of St. Stephen's to be attached to their Society any more unless the venerable building were to benefit in some way from the association. From then on, it seems, the Society was transformed into a benevolent group of philanthropic local businessmen, dedicated to raising funds for the maintenance of the fabric of this historic church, at the heart of the city.

The Society's aims have not changed from that day to this. Every year on the Sunday closest to 17th November, the Society members, in Morning Dress, take part in a commemorative service. Four or five members of the St. Stephen's Ringing Team ring handbells at the service, ringing two bells each. The following Monday the merrymaking tradition of the Society is honoured by a tremendous feast, at which the members change into mock Tudor costume while they sing 'The Golden Days of Good Queen Bess', written in 1788. It is still sung with each verse allotted to a different member. Numerous toasts from the Society's Loving Cup are then proposed and drunk.

The church's Common Room was reopened in 2000 after refurbishment as the "Ringer's Café. It is named in recognition of a donation for the work from the *Antient Society*, and is open at lunchtimes for teas, cakes and homemade light meals.

Details from St. Stephens Parish Office: 0117 9277977 or from bristolrector@aspwebco.net

"They will not be forgotten"

The sound of canon fire reverberates around the quiet city centre on a Sunday morning in Autumn. Two minutes later a military trumpeter sounds the Last Post. Thousands of people who have gathered around The Cenotaph in Colston Avenue are paying their respects to those who lost their lives in the two World Wars and other conflicts.

Members of the uniformed services parade to The Cenotaph where leaders of various faiths, including the Bishop of Bristol, conduct a short service. Members of Parliament, civic leaders and representatives of numerous organisations lay wreaths of poppies around The Cenotaph. The poppy has become the symbol of remembrance since it bloomed widely over the broken battle-fields of Flanders and Picardy in Northern France, in the years after the First World War ended.

This is another occasion to see the Lord Mayor in full regalia accompanied by his swordbearer arrive in a horse-drawn carriage accompanied by a mounted police escort. They are joined at the service by the Lord Lieutenant and High Sheriff of Bristol in their respective uniforms. The service takes place at 11am on Remembrance Sunday every November.

Walking by Water

It could only be a quaint Church of England custom that sees a vicar on an autumn morning trudging through swampy fields, picking his way around cabbage patches and lifting manhole covers. He is putting his best foot forward in memory of the benefactor of the oldest known gift to the people of Redcliffe.

It was in 1190 that Lord Robert de Berkeley, then Lord of the Manor of Bedminster, gave the growing hamlet of Redcliffe a supply of water from his well on a hilltop at Knowle, some two miles away to the south west. From there it flowed through a pipe to an outlet which can still be seen at the corner of Redcliffe Hill and Colston Parade, although it is an inter-war replacement of the original.

Lord Robert decreed that "the church and her ministers were to be allowed to lead the stream of the well over the demesne lands of the tenants, through fence and enclosure and meadow and pasture by a conduit to the church in perpetuity". His gift was typical of the ancient endowments of the English church and was Redcliffe's only source of fresh water for more than 500 years. The Redcliffe clerics shared the water with their parishioners, and a branch pipe supplied the parish of St. Thomas, near Bristol Bridge.

Water ran the full length of the pipe until 1941, when it was damaged by incendiaries dropped by the Luftwaffe on Redcliffe Hill and Spring Street. It now flows into a beautiful commemorative water maze built in Victoria Park by Wessex Water in 1984. The design of the maze was based on the roof boss of St. Mary Redcliffe Church.

Once a year, usually on a Saturday in November, the Vicar of Redcliffe, the churchwardens and parishioners follow the course of the pipe to lay claim to certain endowments. No ordinary trek this. From the well-head located in the middle of a huge allotment site off Daventry Road, Knowle, walkers head downhill through pastureland, along pavements, across a park and eventually onto the church. The route even takes in a private garden. On the way the vicar peers into manholes to check that the pipe is still there.

A series of stone tablets, rather like mini-tomb-stones, mark the course above ground. First timers on the "Pipe Walk" are ceremoniously bumped on one of them near the water maze. Journey's end is at the pipe's outlet, a bronze-inscribed conduit, renewed in 1932 and now under the raised walk that skirts along the west end of the church on Redcliffe Hill.

A newspaper report of the 1930's described the event as a rather grand affair with a band and a dinner laid on in a marquee for the walkers. Both these practices have long been discontinued and those who walk the route today are given coffee and a bun.

Details from St. Mary Redcliffe Parish Office, tel: 0117 9291487

A Society with History

The Society of Merchant Venturers has long shrugged off the accusations of Bristolians that they are a "secret society" of influential businessmen, whose members have manipulated the trade and fortunes of the city – not always to its greater benefit – for hundreds of years. Such allegations arose from the wealth and influence of the Society's members in past times, and their consequent reluctance for publicity. Today the Society has very little wealth itself, although it administers several wealthy trusts, such as the St. Monica Trust, through which the St. Monica's Home for the Elderly on the Downs is maintained. The Society currently has 70 members, of which only three are women - if Margaret Thatcher, who was made an honorary member in 1989, is included.

The society was originally established in 1552 by a royal charter of Edward VI, to try and secure a monopoly on overseas trade for Bristol. Its motto from Horace's First Ode, *indocilis Pauperium Pati* is perhaps an odd choice, as the poet is consistently rude about merchants and their inability to live to a simple life. It refers to the merchant who, even when facing ruin through the loss of his storm-splintered ships, has not been educated to be able to contemplate personal poverty, and begins to build his fortune again. Presumably the Venturers' interpretation was far more straight-faced.

Over the next three hundred years the Merchants helped to build Bristol into a port second only to London, despite the disadvantages of lying several miles inland from the Bristol Channel, with access for ships along a shallow Avon with its difficult tides. The Merchants acted as the port authority and ran the port efficiently; inspecting the quays, cranes, river passages and the pilots who had to bring the ships into the heart of the city. They also financed far-sighted voyages of exploration and trade. The Merchant's Hall was formerly situated on the site of today's Prince Street roundabout, and there was a constant stream of people in and out of the building on harbour business. In the eighteenth century the Merchants broke the trading monopoly of the Royal Africa Company. This established Bristol as the apex of the notorious trade triangle in slaves, tobacco and rum between West Africa and the West Indies, which brought such wealth and elegance to the city, at such human cost.

Until the 1860s it was a pre-requisite for members to have been engaged in seaborne trade. However, Bristol's sea trade declined during the nineteenth century – the tonnage of ships was increasing steadily and the Avon was becoming increasingly difficult to navigate. Some historians have argued the high port charges levied by the Merchants – which were by far the highest in the land – and their reluctance to invest in a new, deeper harbour, contributed to the city's gradual trading stagnation and subsequent eclipse by the far cheaper and more accessible ports of

Liverpool and Glasgow. The Venturers' rules were therefore changed in 1861 to include other city businessmen. The members are now involved not only in Bristol's business life but are also "engaged in useful voluntary service for the community".

The Merchants have long been philanthropically involved with education in the city. In 1595 it administered the Merchant Venturers' Navigation School for the sons of mariners. This developed into the Merchant Venturers' Technical College in 1894, which in turn became part of the University of Bristol Faculty of Engineering in 1909. The Merchants administered funds and trusts for many other educational and charitable establishments, especially for the city's greatest philanthropist, Edward Colston. They administered the Colstons Almshouse on St. Michael's Hill, which was built in 1694, and built the Colston's Girls' School on Cheltenham Road in 1891.

In the seventeenth century the Society acquired the manor and manorial rights of the Sadlier family. In association with the Corporation of Bristol the Society gave the Downs "in perpetuity" to the people of Bristol and now administers the running of the Downs with the City Council.

The Venturers' court of officers still forms the executive body and is elected each year, along with a new Master and Wardens, on November 10 – the date fixed by another charter granted by Charles 1 in 1639. These elections take place in the Society's headquarters, The Merchants' Hall in Clifton, after members have attended their annual service in Bristol Cathedral. From time to time people are invited to become honorary Merchants, and eminent members include the Duke of Edinburgh, Prince Charles, as were three Princes of Wales before him.

Pupils from Colston's Collegiate School at Stapleton and Colston's Girls School in Cheltenham Road join the Merchants for their Charter Day Service. Afterwards they are given buns following a tradition laid down by their founder, Edward Colston.

Access details: Private visits to the beautiful Merchant's Hall in Clifton, which contains a Victorian copy of Queen Elizabeth I's saddle, may be arranged by contacting the Society Secretary, tel: 0117 9733104

Buns, Coins and Flowers mark Colston Day

It is almost impossible to be unaware of the name and fame of the man widely regarded as one of the city's greatest benefactors. The schools, almshouses and charities founded by Edward Colston (1636 - 1721) still bear his name. There are Colston memorial windows in both Bristol Cathedral and St. Mary Redcliffe Church and a dozen or so streets and an office block are named after him. Then there's the Colston concert Hall, All Saints Church off Corn St., which Colston renovated, and in which his tomb is to be found. His statue, by John Cassidy, stands in Colston Avenue, not far from the even more famous but, (in Bristol at least) largely uncelebrated Bristol M.P., the great anti-slavery campaigner and political philosopher Edmund Burke. Colston's statue is adorned by four dolphins at the corners. He had adopted the dolphin as his lucky emblem, it is said, after one of his uninsured ships limped profitably back into port, thanks to a young dolphin which had become wedged in a hole which had threatened to sink the ship. One of Colston's charitable societies is still called the Dolphin Society today.

The irony of Colston's legacy to the city - a city which he left for London in his late teens - is that it was made possible only through his deep involvement in the planning and financing of slave ventures to Africa from Bristol. Colston began his trading fortune by sending ships to the Mediterranean. From 1680 in the middle of his career he became a member of the Royal Africa Company for eighteen years, although he had tried to keep his membership a secret. We can only speculate as to the motives of his philanthropy: perhaps a mixture of gratefulness to the city that had made him so wealthy, a genuine concern for the poor on his doorstep as opposed to those in the holds of his ships, and an atonement to humanity in general. In the latter part of his life he gave away about £100,000, and endowed and beautified Bristol to an incalculable degree. It is fair to say that the citizens of Bristol are still, to this day, unsure of how far to embrace or repudiate him.

Each November 13th marks the anniversary of his birth. First off the mark at one time were the muffled bells of St. Mary Redcliffe Church which began ringing on 12th November, at midnight. They were joined at dawn on the 13th by the bells of other churches throughout the city, and would continue all day. Nowadays a Colston commemoration service is held instead, at St. Mary Redcliffe. It was men from this parish who founded the first of the philanthropic Colston Societies in 1726. The twenty-three founder members of the Colston (Parent) Society subscribed £34. 4s. 0d. for a sermon to be preached "yearly for ever" at the church in memory of the benefactor. The pews are packed with pupils from St. Mary Redcliffe and Temple School and St. Mary Redcliffe Primary School. During the service the President of the Colston Society distributes ten pence coins and large sticky buns to the congregation. This comemmorates Colston's donations of buns to the City's poor.

Colston was also interested in education for poor children, as long as they were from the right sort of religious background. When the governors of the famous Queen Elizabeth's Hospital school for orphan boys refused to exclude the sons of religious Dissidents, Colston withdrew his promise to finance the trebling of the number of pupils, and founded his own school instead. This was Colston's Hospital, at St. Augustine's Place, where the Colston Hall stands today. The school, which still bears his name, later transferred to the Bishop's Palace at Stapleton. The founding principle was firmly stated: to educate in the principles of the Church of England and to maintain and clothe 100 poor boys and place them out to apprentice." In 1891 the trustees of Colston's Hospital also founded a Girls' School in Cheltenham Rd.

It is these girls who commemorate the generosity of their founder on the first Friday in November, and takes place in Bristol Cathedral. The whole school including staff, past staff, girls, 'old girls' and parents attend. Afterwards the Head Girl and Vice Head Girl together with representatives of the Colston societies and pupils from all the Colston schools lay bronze chrysanthemums, Colston's favourite flower, on his ornate tomb in All Saint's Church, off Corn St. Inscribed on the tomb is a list of all the benefactions he made. In former times a nosegay was left on Colston's tomb each Sunday, made up of seasonal flowers. The bouquets were paid for by another Colston legacy specifically for that purpose. Colston's statue in Colston Ave. also receives a bronze chrysanthemum each year.

In the first two weeks of November, members of the Anchor, Dolphin and Grateful societies, which were founded after Colston's death in 1721 to carry on his charitable works, hold their annual collections. The amount collected funds various projects to help the elderly. Fund-raising ends on November 13. The president of each society leads his members, wearing top hats and tails, in procession through the streets to a service at St. Stephen's Church. Members of the Grateful Society used to hold their annual dinner afterwards in the Montague Hotel, which was famed for its turtle soup.

Access Details: Visits to Colston's Tomb, All Saints Church, by special appointment only. All Saints Resource Centre, tel: 0117 9277454 Colston's Almshouses (open to the public on Bristol Open Doors Day, every September)

St. Mary Redcliffe tel: 0117 9291487
St. Stephen's Church tel: 0117 9030976

Marching Maids hold up the City Traffic

Motorists stuck in a traffic jam in the centre of Bristol behind a procession of 600 girls, some wearing cream poke bonnets and red cloaks, can blame John Whitson, a Bristol philanthropist who died more than 300 years ago. The girls are making their way to a church service in honour of the founder of the Red Maids' School.

John Whitson was born in about 1555 in the Forest of Dean in Gloucestershire, and moved to Bristol in around 1570. He became apprenticed to Nicholas Carr, a wine merchant, and eventually took over his profitable trading business by marrying Carr's widow when his former master died. He soon became a wealthy man, served as Mayor of Bristol and was a Member of Parliament.

While sitting as a magistrate in court in November 1626, trying to settle a dispute between two men, one of them stabbed him in the mouth and cheek with a knife. Whitson made a good recovery and as thanks for this he left funds for a sermon to be preached each year at St. Nicholas Church in Baldwin St.

However he died three years later after falling from one of his six horses. One of his several legacies founded the Red Maids' School. He left a grant of £90 a year to provide "a fit convenient dwelling house" for forty girls whose parents were "deceased and decayed". They were to be taught to read English and to "be apparelled in red cloth": hence the Red Maids, although

58

Whitson does not give any clue in his will why he chose this colour. The school was first set up at College Green in 1634. It is now in its own grounds at Westbury on Trym and is the oldest girls school in the country.

The Red Maids mark Founder's Day, normally the third Friday in November, by squeezing into it three church services, starting with Holy Communion at the Lord Mayor's Chapel. Then it is back to school for breakfast. Boarders, along with Sixth-formers, later attend a candlelight service in the medieval crypt of St. Nicholas Church in St. Nicholas St., when they lay wreaths on Whitson's tomb. Afterwards 'day girls' meet up with pupils leaving St. Nicholas Church for the major procession through the city centre to Bristol Cathedral for another service.

The day continues with a formal lunch at the school of steak pie and potatoes for boarders and their guests, followed by the annual prize-giving ceremony when the Lord Mayor or Lady Mayoress cuts the Founder's Day cake.

St. Nicholas Church is closed to the public. Access details from the Bristol Tourist Information Centre, Wildscreen Walk, Harbourside, tel: 0117 9260767

Bristol Cathedral on College Green is open to the public and for church services. Details from the Cathedral office, tel: 0117 9264879

Carols, Choirs and Christingles

During the season of Advent there are many carol concerts and services at schools and churches all over the city, and Bristol's giant civic Christmas Tree is installed each year in St. Stephen's Church, City. Its lights are ceremonially switched on by the Lord Mayor during the evening service at St. Stephen's on the First Advent Sunday.

At the same time hundreds of people turn up at St. Mary Redcliffe Church for its Great Advent Procession by candlelight. Some have arrived an hour early to make sure of a seat. The service starts with the church in total darkness. The sweet voices of the choristers rise to fill the church to its roof as the choral procession moves slowly around the church during the service. Candle-light spreads from member to member of the congregation during the first hymn.

The Christingle Service (probably derived from the German Christ Kindl, or Christ Child) is held in many Bristol churches on the afternoon of Christmas Eve. It has its roots in a ceremony devised by a Moravian pastor for his congregation, who had gathered in the castle room of their Lutheran patron in Marienborn, Germany, in 1747. The Moravians were closely allied to the Lutherans and the Bohemian Hussites, and had recently been expelled from Moravia, in what is now the Czech republic. The children in the congregation were given a lighted candle with a red ribbon tied around it, symbolizing Christ's death for all mankind. It was called a Christingle. The Moravians developed into an influential missionary movement and travelled all over the world, especially to the West Indies and North America. They came to England in the 1740s, and the Christingle custom travelled with them. They influenced the Wesleys and played a major part in the eighteenth century Evangelical Revival, which was especially widespread in Bristol and the West Country.

For children all over Bristol the highlight of the service today is still receiving the Christingle, although the single candle has evolved into an orange with a red ribbon around it, and four cocktail sticks of sweets sticking out at angles. The candle is now inserted in the top of the orange. The orange represents the world, the red ribbons the blood of Christ that saved the world, the sweets are the fruits of the world, and the candle, the light of Christ.

Access Details: St. Stephen's Advent Service, tel. Parish Office 0117 9277977

St. Mary Redcliffe Advent Service, tel. Parish Office 0117 9291487

The Vicar's Christmas Feast

Bristol is a great city for its charities and philanthropists. Many benefactors were conscious of the plight of the poor and aged and established almshouses for them. Some of the houses still exist, one of the oldest being Dr. White's.

The Reverend Dr. Thomas White, the son of a clothier, was born in the old Temple Parish of Bristol. He was educated at Magdalen College, Oxford, and trained for Holy Orders. The Rev. White had an impressive career in the church, holding some lucrative positions, including that of Rector of St. Dunstan's-in-the-West in London's Fleet Street for nearly 50 years. He also served as a Prebendary of St. Paul's Cathedral, a Canon of Christ Church, Oxford, and was a Canon at St. George's Chapel, Windsor.

In 1613 Dr. White set up Temple Hospital in Temple Street, not far from his birthplace, with room for ten people - eight men and two widows - whom he selected. His original deed for the hospital states that the dwellings were for "the finding, sustenation and relief of poor, needy or impotent people". During his lifetime Dr. White governed the hospital himself.

He died in London aged 74 and in his will set out instructions for a feast to be held at the hospital every December 21 - the Feast Day of the Apostle Thomas and the date of his own birthday. Dr. White left forty shillings for the feast and in his will stipulated that special pewter plate be used for the occasion. There were also instructions about the menu, which included a baron of beef and apple pie flavoured with a quince. As a further

Christmas present each inhabitant received a roll of cloth and sufficient money for turning it into a garment.

The dinner still takes place, and the relevant parts of Dr. White's will are still read to the assembled guests, residents of the almshouse, its trustees and the Lord Mayor of Bristol, as stipulated by the benefactor nearly four hundred years ago.

The original almshouse was near Temple Church, but was rebuilt several times. In 1968 it was demolished and replaced by 18 bungalows set around a neat courtyard in Prewett Street, Redcliffe, which is known as Dr. White's Close.

Bristol's Fairs and Markets

Outside the 18th century Exchange Buildings in Corn Street, built by John Wood the elder who did so much to beautify Bath, stand the famous Bristol Nails. Merchants placed their money on the four bronze, flat-topped pillars to seal their bargains. Hence the saying "Paying on the nail". Bristol was not the only city in England with this custom, but it is only in Corn Street that the nails have been preserved. The nails date from the 16th century. The presidents of the Colston Societies also symbol-ically exchange cheques on the nails when they launch their annual fund-raising appeals.

Today the top of Corn Street is the site of the weekly famers' market, every Wednesday morning, where locally grown and organic meat, cheese, garden produce, cakes, bread and preserves of excellent quality are sold to the public.

At the bottom of Corn St., in Broad Quay, the Bristol Christmas Market has been held for the past few years, and also looks set to become a tradition. Stall owners, previously from Germany, more recently from France, sell local produce, Christmas decorations and crafts.

 ## Bristol Fairs in the past

Fairs once played an important part in city life, particularly in ports such as Bristol. Until the early decades of the twentieth century many street markets were still held in the old central streets of Bristol, but after the Blitz and further judicious levelling and reconstruction by the post war planners, many of the old sites vanished, with only the street names remaining to offer an echo of the past.

July saw the Colt Fair at the Cattle Market. The venue for the Leather Fairs was the Corn Exchange on the second Wednesday in March and September. At one time, it has been said, more tanned leather was sold during these fairs than at any other place in the British Isles. Wool Fairs were also held on these days and were well attended by dealers and fellmongers from the Midlands and North. The Cattle Market, covering four acres of land around Temple Meads, to the east of Bath Bridge, was opened in February 1830. Some of the land was subsequently acquisitioned to extend the railway station, so the market was reconstructed by the Great Western and Midland Railway Boards in 1874 at a cost of £10,000. The area incorporated a house for the clerk of the market and was owned by the Corporation. The Hide Market was in

St. Thomas Street. The building still stands and is now the Fleece and Firkin pub.

Until 1838, fairs were held annually at the Great Gardens, a remnant of the lands possessed by Bristol Castle. This fair was in March and lasted ten days, as did the fair which was held in St James' churchyard every September. By 1905 the Fair no longer took place in the churchyard, but coal could still be bought there. It was separated from the burial ground by iron railings. During the same period, hay and straw were still sold in the Haymarket nearby.

The Cheese Market was held in Union Street every Wednesday and Friday. It was also used as a meat, vegetable and fruit market. It was an impressive structure which partially survived the Blitz, but was swept away in the 1950s in favour of modern shops. The Corn and Flour Market was held, naturally, at the Corn Exchange and this took place every Tuesday and Thursday. The Fish Market in Nicholas Street, which had formerly been the city meat market, was a daily event. Now not one butcher remains.

The High Street Market, which now blends into St Nicholas Market opened on April 14th 1849. It was occupied on Wednesdays and Saturdays by dealers in butter, cheese, eggs, poultry and bacon. Market gardeners from the areas surrounding the city would sell from stalls here on a daily basis. Whith the re-introduction of the Farmer's Market every Wednesday in nearby Corn St., this is one tradition at least that has been revived.

The impressive Corn Exchange between Corn St. and St. Nicholas St. now contains the permanent St. Nicholas market, selling not only cooked and fresh food, but also all manner of crafts, jewellery, memorabilia, second hand books, records and leatherwear.

Bibliography

Apparelled in Red by Jean **Vanes** *Governors of The Red Maids' School, revised edition 1992*

Bristol Heritage *Redcliffe Press in association with Bristol Religious Heritage Group, 1991*

The Best of Bristol Times *Bristol Evening Post, 1998 - 2003*

Canynges Society Gazette *Various editions*

Children's Bristol *Redcliffe Press, 1976*

St. Mary Redcliffe Church Parish Magazine *Various editions*

St. Mark's: The Lord Mayor's Chapel by Alan **Canterbury** *Bristol City Council*

St. Stephen's Church, City, Parish Magazine *Various editions*

The Street Names of Bristol, 2nd Ed. by Veronica **Smith** *Broadcast Books 2002*

Secret Underground Bristol *Broadcast Books 2002*

The First Two Hundred Years *The Bristol Law Society, 1970*

The Story of Old Bristol by E. M. **Habgood**, 2nd edition produced by Industrial Arts (Bristol) 1955?

While We Have Time by J.R. **Avery**, 1990

Church magazines 1930 - present day

Other local titles from Broadcast Books

Available from local bookshops. In case of difficulty please contact Catherine Mason on 0117 9238891 or send a cheque plus £1.00 postage and packing to Broadcast Books, c/o Clifton Bookshop, 84 Whiteladies Rd., Bristol BS8 2QP

Bristol: Fresh Perspectives
Original Photographs *by* Huntley Hedworth *and* Sally Mundy

November 2003

304 pages   288 colour photographs £25.00 isbn: 1874092 990
The beautiful, the vibrant, the unexpected, the tranquil: this extensive photographic essay celebrates the many aspects of this thriving and changing city, with over 300 specially commissioned photographs by Bristol photographers Sally Mundy and Huntley Hedworth. As well as the familiar panoramas of Brunel's Suspension Bridge and famous Clifton terraces here are also the changing city riverscapes, the culturally energetic areas of Easton, Bedminster and St. Pauls, the people, the architecture, the abundant green, in grand scale and in touching detail. Extended captions link the photographs which combine to offer the widest photographic perspective of Bristol published to date.

Detail from frieze, Kingsweston House, Bristol

The Street Names of Bristol: their Meanings and Origins

by Veronica Smith

2nd edition

isbn: 1874092 90 7 pbk 246 pages £11.95

Following the sell-out success of the first edition, here is the second edition, substantially enlarged and revised to include hundreds of pieces of new information that were sent in by readers. Do you know why Zed Alley is so-called? What happened on Air Balloon Hill? Or why Ernest Barker should have a road named after him? Bristol's street names - ancient and modern - are a wonderful source of history, legend and local tradition, from Roman way to Millennium Mile. Veronica Smith reveals many new stories lying behind the naming of Bristol's streets: here are kings, philanthropists, healers, saints and murderers, milkmen, builders and millionaires, as well as the echoes of long-forgotten landscape features. The Street names of Bristol is an invaluable resource for local historians, and a wonderful read for anyone who has ever wondered what a street name means and why it was chosen.

St. Michaels Hill, circa 1910

The Old Inns of Bristol
by Grace Cooper,
Maurice Fells *and* Veronica Smith
40 maps and Illustrations by Lorna Rankin

November 2003

isbn: 1874092 97 4176 pages £10.95 pbk
The existing inns of the old port city of Bristol reveal much about its history, and many have intriguing tales to tell. Which pub has a door covered in human skin? Which watering hole near the shopping centre has a ghost? Where are the oldest licensed premises in the city, and what plots have been hatched there? In this fascinating trawl, the authors tell the stories behind Bristol's oldest surviving inns, and revisit the shades of famous, now vanished venues when inns also stabled horses, bedded down their travelling customers and stocked their ponds with turtles to feed them. The humbler working men's taverns on the street corners of Bristol's many different trade areas are also revisited, and their names and origins explained. Another fascinating contribution to the history of Bristol .

Secret Underground Bristol and Beyond
(2nd revised edition)
by Sally Watson

isbn: 1 874092 95 8 pbk 144 pages illustrated £14.95
Following the extraordinary success of the first edition of this book, Broadcast Books and the Bristol Junior Chamber of Commerce have combined to produce a second, revised and enlarged edition which takes in much new material, including never before described secret tunnel systems under Coombe Down, Bath, and many new maps. The book is a voyage of discovery, not only leading you into the eerie underworld beneath our streets and revealing these unsuspected spaces, but also telling many fascinating human stories behind the.m. From professional hermits to eccentric industrialists, dozens of extraordinary characters bring the subterranean city of Bristol and its environs to life. The book links up with the Open Days of Bristol, enabling readers to actually visit many of the sites described.

"... this is a book full of delectable delights... READ ON...READ ON!"

Lucinda Lambton

Where Kingcups Grew
A West Country Childhood
by Lewis Wilshire

Hardback illustrated £10.95   144 pages

Where Kingcups Grew by Lewis Wilshire is the swan song of one of the West Country's best loved writers. Originally written over many years for the Bristol Evening Post, Lewis Wilshire compiled this personal collection of delightful tales of his Bristol childhood. Here is the long-vanished landscape of streams, meadows and wildlife from eighty years ago, a landscape which now lies beneath the concrete confines of the city. Also recalled with affection and poignancy is a cavalcade of eccentric friends and relations. Beautifully written, these recollections will become a classic of their kind.

"A classic."
Bristol Evening Post

The Granary Club: the Rock Years 1969 – 1988
by Al Read & Terry Brace

September 2003

isbn:1874092 82 6 Pbk £12.95 Over 200 illustrations 288 pages

From the tail-end of the Sixties and into the Seventies this beautiful 19th century grain warehouse in Bristol's historic dock area became a hot-bed of rock music and outrageously liberal attitudes that is still remembered fondly by its acolytes as "The Old Granary". In *The Granary Club - The Rock Years* former manager Al Read has collected a chronological record of the many bands that played at the club (and how much they were paid), as many torn photographs and fragments of graphics and as many anecdotes as were capable of being pieced together. Here is the group of misfits who called themselves Plastic Dog and the musicians, artists, photographers, writers and general music freaks who grew out of the place. In fact virtually everyone apart from David Bowie and Pink Floyd tripped on the steps of the tiny wooden stage at one time or another. Read it and weep for the years of your youth!